The wonder of teachers

C.R.Gibson®
FINE GIFTS SINCE 1870

All images © Hulton Getty Picture Collection.
Picture research by Jon Wright.
Design by Keith Jackson.
All text, unless otherwise attributed, by Jonathan Bicknell.

Developed by Publishing Services Corporation, Nashville, Tennessee.

Published by C. R. Gibson®
C. R. Gibson® is a registered trademark of Thomas Nelson, Inc.
Nashville, Tennessee 37214
Printed and bound by L. Rex Printing Company Limited, China

ISBN: 0-7667-6757-4
UPC: 0-82272-46687-6
GB4154

The wonder of teachers

"School days are the best days of your life!"

"Are you sitting
comfortably?

Then we'll begin."

"Teachers affect **eternity**; they can **never** tell where **their** influence **stops.**"

"You helped me believe in myself – because seeing is believing."

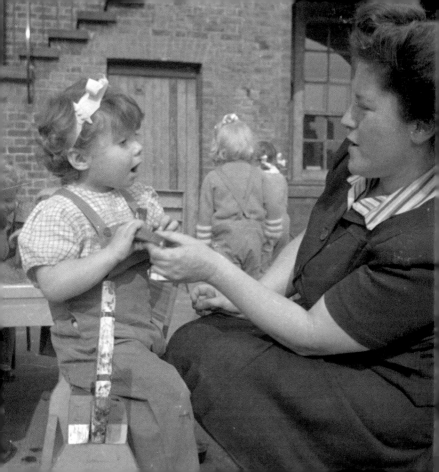

"Whatever I said, you listened."

"To **you** a

picture

is **worth** a

1000

words..."

"... And every
picture
tells a
story."

"The larger the knowledge, the greater the wonder."

"I keep **six** honest serving men. They **taught** me all I knew. Their names are What and Why and When, and How and Where and Who."

– Rudyard Kipling

"When pain and **anguish** wring the brow, a **ministering** angel **thou.**"

– Sir Walter Scott

"Your tireless efforts on our behalf did not go unobserved."

"No more English, no more French, no more sitting on the old school bench."

"Without you, I might never have tried..."

"...And pleasing you made my heart sing."

"Girls scream, boys shout,
dogs bark,
school's out!"

– W H Davies